D1327767

DOGS

DOGS
FAITHFUL FRIENDS

Kirsty Seymour-Ure

RYLAND
PETERS
& SMALL

LONDON NEW YORK

Senior Designer   Paul Tilby

Editor   Sophie Bevan

Editorial Assistant   Miriam Hyslop

Location Research Manager   Kate Brunt

Production   Patricia Harrington

Art Director   Gabriella Le Grazie

Publishing Director   Alison Starling

Special Photography   Chris Tubbs

First published in the United Kingdom in 2001
by Ryland Peters & Small
Kirkman House, 12–14 Whitfield Street,
London W1T 2RP
www.rylandpeters.com

10 9 8 7 6 5 4 3 2

Text © Kirsty Seymour-Ure 2001
Design and photographs
© Ryland Peters & Small 2001

Printed and bound in China by Toppan Printing Co.

ISBN 1 84172 126 3

A CIP record for this book is available from
the British Library.

contents

faithful friends

Dogs are justly famed for their faithfulness and enduring loyalty. They take delight in human contact. And they are the most generous and ungrudging of friends.

The world is full of dogs - dogs of all shapes and aspects, dogs of such an amazing variety of size and style that it is hard to believe that a bouncy little Jack Russell and a huge Great Dane belong to the same species. There are now more than four hundred distinct breeds and, while many are kept for work, most modern dogs are valued household companions. Yet in spite of their enormous variety they all have a common ancestor: the wolf.

Dogs and humans go back a long way together. They probably gravitated naturally into each other's company some twelve thousand years ago - the dogs no doubt attracted by the chance to beg a few scraps and the humans

THE FIRST FRIEND

glad to have a protective creature about. The dog is thus our oldest domestic companion. Hunting ally, herder of flocks, guardian of the camp: dogs were willing workmates and then became an integral part of the family circle - so much so that many families now feel incomplete without a dog's benign presence.

Small, medium or large; curly-coated or smooth; plain or patterned; quiet and docile or loud and vigorous; among the myriad different breeds there are dogs to suit all tastes and styles.

GREAT AND SMALL

Despite the variety of size and form and the wide-ranging nature of their talents, all dogs are basically the same: they are social animals and speak the same language all over the world. A Welsh farm collie can happily pass the time  of day with a spoilt French poodle, while well-groomed city setters will play and frolic among their country relatives with the greatest of ease. Dogs are naturally friendly, and it is this that makes them adapt so well to family life, as they transfer their pack loyalties to their human companions. You just need to make certain that everyone knows who's the leader of the pack.

sleek sloths

Dogs like their creature comforts and happily spend a large portion of their day drowsing. They won't say no to a soft cushion, but the floor is as good a place as any.

Some dogs are so relaxed that, given the chance, they will sleep anywhere, anytime. Deep sleep is interspersed with lighter dozing, when the least noise will make the dog spring awake.

There is a deep and genuine bond of affection that exists between a hound and its human owner, whether the dog is a working assistant or a friendly presence in the home. There are times when the gaze of your canine companion really does melt your heart. The affectionate and trusting look on that gentle face is irresistible – those appealing chocolate eyes! – even when your dog is gazing up at you from the immaculate white sofa that he knows all too well is strictly prohibited.

Dogs are essentially built for hunting. A loping gait, along with great stamina, enables them to cover a very long distance and then to accelerate with a final burst of speed. Some dogs are especially elegant when running. Like the greyhound, the whippet has a particular gait that makes it appear to fly over the ground. With its sleek coat and refined face, it has a dancer's muscled grace even when drowsing.

DREAMS OF FLYING

Running is not the forte of all dogs; short-legged terriers and hounds were bred to hunt small game underground. Small as they are, these bright-eyed dogs are feisty and alert; you may wish they spent a bit more time asleep!

SLEEPING SMALL

luxurious loungers

Some dogs are naturally indolent; some dogs are inherently boisterous. But it is a rare dog that does not enjoy a good snooze on a comfortable chair when no one is looking.

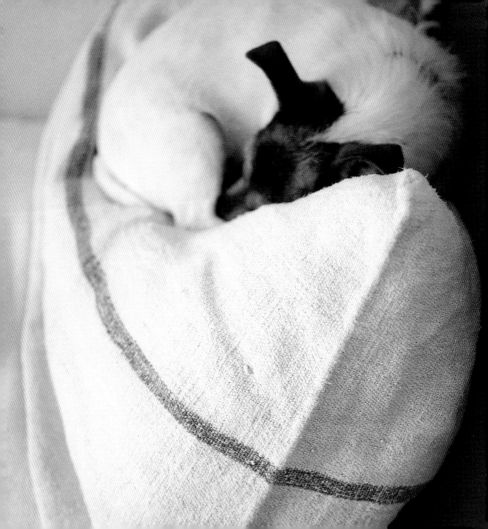

Along with their many other skills, dogs possess a highly evolved talent for lazing about - not always asleep, but relishing what they clearly believe to be an essential and well-earned rest. Despite an owner's exhortations that he get up and do something useful, a dog thus reposing is unlikely to stir unless thoroughly convinced that it will be worth his while.

DO NOT DISTURB

Do dogs roam free in the world of dreams, chasing dream-rabbits; or is sleep simply a chance to relax away from the demands of a busy life? Dogs can be quite active in their sleep,

CHASING DREAMS

twitching, moving their legs and even barking, and it seems likely they are dreaming. A half-awake dog, his ears flicking back and forth scanning for sounds imperceptible to humans, seems lost in philosophical contemplation, although he is probably just wondering whether it is tea-time yet.

TO THE MANNER BORN

Dog hairs on the sofa (in fact, dog hairs everywhere) are a reality of life for dog owners. Dogs are by nature eager to please and dislike offending their owners, but sometimes the lure of a comfortable seat is just too much to bear. And when a dog looks so much at home on his chosen throne, who would deny him his moments of lordly luxury?

... the most precious and valuable
possession of mankind

Theodorus Gaza (1398–1478)

Dogs like plenty of exercise to keep them healthy, and sane. A penned-up or housebound dog chases her tail, gnaws the furniture or bites the newspaper deliverer. Certain dogs, such as the intelligent and energetic collie, need more exercise than others. Tired out after a hard day herding sheep, a vigorous hike or a long run in the local park, a dog sleeps deeply and

SLEEP OF THE JUST

contentedly. She might just manage to wag her tail and open her eyes for a second if you stroke her, but then sleep takes over again, replenishing her energy for tomorrow's exertions.

standing guard

All dogs have a highly developed instinct to protect. Large or small, they will defend loved ones, their possessions and their territory from real or imagined danger.

The innate tendency of dogs to defend and to protect is so pronounced that guard dogs feature prominently in religion and myth. The entrance to Hades, the ancient Greek underworld, was guarded by a fearsome

BEWARE OF THE DOG

many-headed hound called Cerberus. In pharaonic Egypt a dog-headed god, Anubis, was the protector of tombs. Today's real-life watchdogs may be highly trained professionals – or simply amateurs proving their loyalty.

Tiny, deceptively fragile-looking 'lion dogs' serve as sacred sentinels in the Buddhist temples of Tibet, but in general, watchdogs are drawn from the larger breeds. On a kind of inbuilt principle, many dogs are wary of strangers, and this enhances their protectiveness towards the members of their 'pack'. Only when newcomers have earned her trust will a dog drop her guard. Ever vigilant, and ready to bark a warning, she carefully controls access to the inmost sanctuary.

... by night he watcheth faithfully

Joachim Camerarius (1500–1574)

Size in itself has no effect on the ferociousness or courage of a dog: small dogs can be extremely fierce, while many of the larger breeds are renowned as gentle giants. Despite the protective instinct, some dogs can not disguise the friendliness of their

PLAY WITH ME

nature. Strangers are welcomed with a brief show of barking that quickly becomes a welter of friendly licks, or examined with a soft, enquiring gaze that practically begs them to step inside. These are sweet, unsuspicious, affectionate dogs who would happily be friends with the whole world.

up to mischief

Torn between a desire to please its master by being good and an urge to make mischief, a dog will often choose the latter. Sometimes having fun is just irresistible.

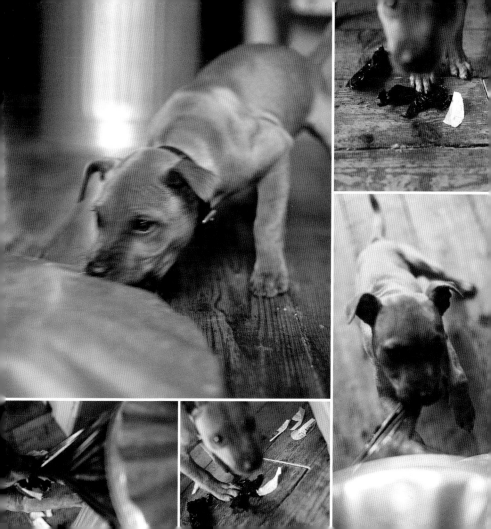

Not only are dogs highly intelligent but they are also naturally inclined to obey, especially once their (lowly) position in the social hierarchy of the family is clearly established. Their willingness makes training them relatively easy, and they certainly know when they are being naughty. Now and again even the best behaved of dogs seems to relish letting go, breaking the rules - and hang the consequences.

Essentially a dog's prime yearning is to please his master; but other longings, such as that set up by a plate of iced cakes, are never far

behind. Many dogs will have no hesitation whatsoever in succumbing to temptation, even in front of their owner's eyes, so great is their desire; well-trained, obedient types may wait a little longer, hoping that virtuous self-restraint and sad, pleading looks will bring their own reward.

PLEASE, PLEASE, PLEASE . . .

Curiosity may have killed the cat, but it got the dog into trouble too. Dogs are impetuous creatures and act without thinking. Usually the danger is not to themselves but to your house and things; fragile ornaments are regularly destroyed or half-full mugs spilled by

THRILLS AND SPILLS

a single sweep of an overexcited tail. Dogs are interested in everything that goes on in their home, and letting even a small one loose when the decorators are in is akin to madness, unless you are after some special paint effects.

CREDITS

Endpapers Polke; **1** Rolf; **2** Stratford; **3** Max; **4–5** Ben; **6** Milo; **9** photo Tom Leighton/Inca; **10l** Bill, **10tr** Stratford, **10br** Merlin; **11t** Jill, **11c** photo Christopher Drake, **11b** Bruno; **13** Blue at Ochre, London; **14** Jenny, **14tr** photo Chris Everard; **14br** Enzo; **15** photo Catherine Gratwicke; **16** photo Alan Williams; **17** photo Francesca Yorke/Lily; **18–19** photo Andrew Wood/Chelsea Loft Apartment in New York designed by The Moderns; **21** Merlin; **22–23** photo Andrew Wood/John Cheim's apartment in New York; **24–25** Milo; **26–27** Blue at Ochre, London; **28–29** Polke; **30** Ben; **33** photo Andrew Wood/Jane Collins of Sixty 6 in Marylebone High Street, home in central London; **34–35** photo Andrew Wood/Inca; **36–37** Rolf; **38–39** photo Chris Everard; **40** Bill; **42** photo Tom Leighton; **45** Dave; **46** photo Francesca Yorke; **47** photo Andrew Wood; **48-49** photo Andrew Wood/Michael Benevento Orange Group; **51** Stratford; **52** Ben; **55** Stratford; **56** photo Andrew Wood/Spot; **57** photo Andrew Wood/Inca; **58–59** Milo; **61** Polke; **62** Stratford.

The publisher would like to thank everyone who allowed us to photograph their dogs. Special thanks to Elspeth, Claudia and Kate, Ivan, Danielle and Richard, Clare, Lucy and Perou, Harriet (at Ochre, 22 Howie Street, London SW11 4AS. www.ochre.net. tel. 020 7223 8888), Debbie and John, Phil and Caroline, Peter and Maureen, Chris and Jenny, and Karen.